MW01251562

Ladybug Landing

Bible Book

Bug Safari

A SPECIAL SHEPHERD

(adapted from 1 Samuel 16:1-13)

[Samuel] was a prophet—that means he told people important messages from God. One day, God told [Samuel] to go to Bethlehem and visit a man named Jesse. God was choosing a new [king] for his people, and the new [king] would be one of Jesse's [sons].

Jesse had many [sons]. [Samuel] looked at each of the [sons], listening for God to tell him if *this one* would be the new [king]. But for each of the [sons], [Samuel] said to Jesse, "The Lord has not chosen this one." Finally [Samuel] had seen all of Jesse's [sons].

"Are these all of the [sons] you have?" [Samuel] asked.

"There is still the youngest," Jesse said, "but he's watching over the [sheep]."

So [Samuel] sent for young [David]. When [David] came, God told [Samuel], "He is the one."

[Samuel] blessed [David]. God knew that someday [David], the little shepherd boy, would be a mighty [king].

[Samuel] – Samuel   [king] – king   [sons] – sons

[sheep] – sheep   [David] – David

3

HELPING HANDS

(adapted from 1 Samuel 17)

[David]'s [brothers] went to fight some bad men called the [Philistines]. One of the [Philistines] was a giant man named [Goliath]. Each day for many days [Goliath] came out of the [Philistines] camp and shouted mean things to God's people, the Israelites. But the Israelites were scared to fight big, mean [Goliath], and they all ran from him!

One day, [David] came to bring his [brothers] some food. He heard the terrible things that [Goliath] said about God's people. That made [David] angry! He wanted to fight [Goliath] so that [Goliath] would know how powerful God is! But [David] was just a boy. How could a boy fight a giant?

[David] picked up some smooth [stones] from the stream. He took one of the [stones] and put it in his sling. [David] said, "You come at me with a sword and spear… but I come at you in the name of the Lord. God will help me defeat you!"

[David] swung his sling, and then he let go! The stone flew through the air and hit [Goliath] right in the middle of his forehead. The mean giant fell down dead!

But [David] didn't beat [Goliath] all by himself. God helped [David] do a big job—even though [David] was little!

[David] – David   [brothers] – brothers

[Philistines] – Philistines   [Goliath] – Goliath   [stones] – stones

BEST FRIENDS

(adapted from 1 Samuel 18–20)

[David] and [Jonathan] were best friends. [Jonathan] even gave [David] some special presents—his [robe], [sword], [bow], and [belt].

[Jonathan] was the son of King [Saul]. [Saul] didn't like [David]. [Saul] was afraid that people liked [David] better, so [Saul] wanted to hurt [David]. It was dangerous for [David] to live near [Saul].

"I'll find out if my father wants to hurt you," [Jonathan] told [David]. "If he does, I'll send a secret message to tell you to run far away."

[Jonathan] did what he said he would, and he found out that King [Saul] really *did* want to kill [David]. [Jonathan] shot arrows through the air as a secret message, and [David] knew that he had to go far away where he would be safe. The friends were so sad that they wouldn't see each other anymore. But [Jonathan] had been a good friend— he had saved [David]'s life.

[David] – David [Jonathan] – Jonathan [robe] – robe [sword] – sword
[bow] – bow [belt] – belt [Saul] – Saul

ALiVE, ALiVE!

(adapted from Mark 15:1–16:8)

 is God's Son. He came to earth to show how much God us.

said that God would take away all of the bad things we've done. Lots and lots of

people loved . They followed him and listened to him teach about God. They

were that God could forgive our sins!

But some people were angry and jealous. They thought that wasn't telling

the truth. So to make be quiet, they hurt him, and then they killed him.

Those mean people hung on a until he died. That was a day.

After died, his body was put in a , which is like a cave. Three days

later, some of 's friends came to the . But the big stone that had

covered up the opening to the had been rolled away…and

wasn't there! was alive! God is stronger than death, so God made

live again! That was a day!

 died and rose again so that we could live with God in heaven forever.

God forgives our sins because he us so much!

ABIGAIL MAKES PEACE

(adapted from 1 Samuel 25:1-35)

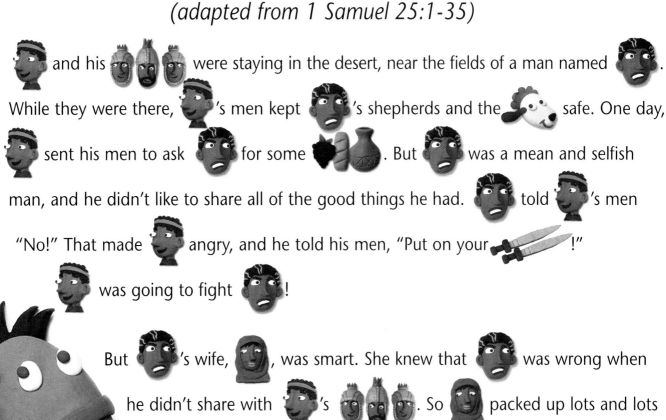

[David] and his [army] were staying in the desert, near the fields of a man named [Nabal].

While they were there, [David]'s men kept [Nabal]'s shepherds and the [sheep] safe. One day,

[David] sent his men to ask [Nabal] for some [food and drink]. But [Nabal] was a mean and selfish

man, and he didn't like to share all of the good things he had. [Nabal] told [David]'s men

"No!" That made [David] angry, and he told his men, "Put on your [swords]!"

[David] was going to fight [Nabal]!

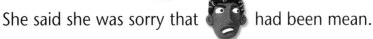

But [Nabal]'s wife, [Abigail], was smart. She knew that [Nabal] was wrong when

he didn't share with [David]'s [army]. So [Abigail] packed up lots and lots

of [food and drink]. She took all of those good things to [David] and his men.

When [Abigail] found [David], she bowed down and gave him the [food and drink].

She said she was sorry that [Nabal] had been mean.

[David] was surprised! He told his men to put their [swords]

away. [David] said to [Abigail], "Praise God for sending you today!

You have saved your household!"

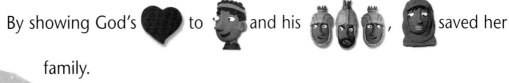

By showing God's [love] to [David] and his [army], [Abigail] saved her

family.

[David] – David   [army] – army   [Nabal] – Nabal   [sheep] – sheep   [food and drink] – food and drink

[swords] – swords   [Abigail] – Abigail   [love] – love

11

Bible Story: Samuel anoints David (1 Samuel 16:1-13).

Bible Verse: "O Lord, you have searched me and you know me" (Psalm 139:1).

DAY 1

GOD KNOWS US.

Name: _____

MUDDY MUNCHiES

Help your child use soap and water to wash out a small plastic flowerpot, and use aluminum foil to plug up any drainage holes. Then let your child spoon in chocolate pudding, along with a few gummy worms. Put two chocolate sandwich cookies into a resealable sandwich bag. Close the bag, then let your preschooler smash the cookies into something that looks like dirt. Sprinkle the cookies on top of the pudding to make a delightful, delicious "dirt" dessert!

Before enjoying the treat, pray: **Dear God, thank you for knowing and loving us—no matter what we look like on the outside. We're glad that your love is sweet and good. In Jesus' name, amen.**

PEEKABOO PLATES

Get out paper plates, crayons, and other craft items such as stickers, glue, buttons, and yarn. You and your child can draw silly faces on the paper plates to make masks.

Now you and your preschooler can each hide behind a mask as you sing the following song to the tune of "Frère Jacques."

Parent: **Where is [name]? Where is [name]?**

Child: **Here I am!** (Have your child move the mask away from his or her face.) **Here I am!**

Parent: **God knows you and loves you—He's always thinking of you!**

Child: **God knows me! God knows me!**

Bug BEATS

God Looks at Our Hearts

(sung to the tune of "Row, Row, Row Your Boat")

God looks at our hearts,
At our hearts each day.
He doesn't care how we look;
Love God and obey!

Bug BuDDiES

Today your child learned that when a stick bug isn't moving, it looks just like a little stick—even though it's really a bug! Your preschooler also learned that even when David was just a young boy, God knew that David would be a great king one day. That's because God knows us! Ask your child:

- **Why do you think God knows us so well?**
- **What are some things you know about God?**

Copyright © Group Publishing, Inc. www.groupvbs.com

DAY 2

GOD HELPS US.

Bible Story: David defeats Goliath (1 Samuel 17).
Bible Verse: "I lift up my eyes to the hills—where does my help come from? My help comes from the Lord, the Maker of heaven and earth" (Psalm 121:1-2).

Name: _____

DAVID DEFEATS GOLIATH.

GIVE ME A LIFT!

You've probably heard of ants on a raft (raisins on a graham cracker) or ants on a log (raisins on celery), but those must be lazy ants! Ants are buff bugs that can do big things! Give your child a handful of chocolate chip "ants." Remind your child that ants may be little, but they can lift fifty times their body weight—that's a big job! Let your child balance a graham cracker on top of four chocolate chips, as if ants are carrying a raft. Add some food items, such as dry cereal, on top of the raft to represent "weighty problems." Take turns with your child, and each time you add a piece of food, tell a problem that you need God's help with. Pray with your preschooler, and thank God for helping us with every problem. Then gobble up the raft before the ants walk away with it!

BUG BEATS

God Is Mighty
(sung to the tune of "Twinkle, Twinkle, Little Star")

God is mighty
   (flex right arm);
God is strong. *(Flex left arm.)*
I will praise God all day long.
   (Raise arms, then move them out to the sides.)
God will help me do great things
   (give two thumbs up)
That is why I praise and sing.
   (Cup hands around mouth.)

God is mighty *(flex right arm);*
God is strong. *(Flex left arm.)*
I will praise God all day long.
   (Raise arms, then move them out to the sides.)

Bug Buddies

Today your child learned that even though ants are tiny, they can do big things. (Did you know that an ant can lift fifty times its own body weight?) Your child was reminded that David was small, but God helped David defeat a mean giant!

Copyright © Group Publishing, Inc. www.groupvbs.com

DAY 3

GOD IS OUR FRIEND.

Bible Story: David and Jonathan are friends (1 Samuel 18–20).

Bible Verse: "The Lord is my shepherd, I shall not be in want" (Psalm 23:1).

Name: _____

FRIENDLY FASHION

Preschoolers love getting gifts! Remind your child that Jonathan gave David some special gifts—a robe, a tunic, a bow, a sword, and a belt. Then grab an old pillowcase, a pair of scissors, and some markers or fabric paints. It's time to make a "royal robe" to remember the gifts that Jonathan gave to David.

Cut the pillowcase up the middle, from the open end to the closed end. Then cut about three inches to each side of the center cut to make a place for your child's head and neck. Next cut out armholes on both sides. Finally, let your child go wild…with color, that is! Your preschooler will have a blast decorating the robe with pictures of friends. Remind your child that God is our very best friend!

BUG BEATS

Ten Little Friends
(sung to the tune of "Ten Little Indians")

One little, two little, three little friends,
Four little, five little, six little friends,
Seven little, eight little, nine little friends,
Ten little friends praise God! *(Raise hands and wiggle fingers.)*

A HONEY OF A SNACK

Of course our bee buddies make sweet, sticky, scrumptious honey. What better reminder than honey that God is a friend who sticks with us all the time! Help your child make two slices of toast. Get out a heart-shaped cookie cutter, and let your child cut the toast into two heart shapes. One heart will represent your child, and the other will represent God. Help your preschooler drizzle honey on the heart-shaped toast, then stick the pieces together like a sandwich. Talk about how God is our best friend because he loves us and never leaves us.

BUG BUDDIES

Today your child learned that bees are our bug buddies, in spite of those dangerous stingers! Your preschooler discovered that bees help flowers grow, and bees work hard to find food for their hive families. In a similar way, God is always busy watching over us, providing for us, and helping us grow. God is a sweet friend to have!

Copyright © Group Publishing, Inc. www.groupvbs.com

DAY 4

GOD FORGIVES US.

Bible Story: **Jesus dies on the cross and rises again** (Mark 15:1–16:8).

Bible Verse: **"Create in me a pure heart, O God, and renew a steadfast spirit within me"** (Psalm 51:10).

Name: _____

IN A PINCH

Take a break from doing laundry, and put those clothespins to use for something *fun* for a change! All you need is a clean coffee filter, a clothespin, and some watercolor markers. Flatten out the coffee filter, and let your child use markers to color it. (For extra fun, let your child lightly spray the filter with water and watch the colors mix together!) Then let your child scrunch the filter together in the middle to make wings. Pinch a clothespin on the scrunched spot to make the butterfly's body. Explain that butterflies can remind us of Jesus because just as caterpillars come out of cocoons, Jesus rose from the grave!

BUG BEATS

God Still Loves Me
(sung to the tune of "Jesus Loves Me")

God still loves me when I sin,
No matter how wrong I've been.
God wants me to choose his way.
God forgives me when I pray.
Yes, God forgives me.
Yes, God forgives me.
Yes, God forgives me,
Because he loves me so.

CHANGE YOUR HEART

Bring out a bag of unpopped popcorn and tell your child that you're ready for a snack. (Some preschoolers will dig right in, while others will look at you as if you've lost your mind!) Taste a few kernels, and talk about how they're hard to chew and don't taste very good. Ask your child what would make this snack better. Explain that the kernels need to change before you can enjoy them. While you pop the popcorn, tell your child that *we* need to change before we can live with God forever in heaven. Point out that God's forgiveness washes our hearts clean so that we can be with God forever!

BUG BUDDIES

Today your child learned that butterflies don't start out looking so great—they start out as crawly caterpillars! But inside the cocoon, a caterpillar's body changes into something amazing...a butterfly! Just as a caterpillar changes and has new life, God's forgiveness changes our hearts and gives us new life.

Copyright © Group Publishing, Inc. www.groupvbs.com

Bible Story: Abigail makes peace with David
(1 Samuel 25:1-35).

DAY 5

Bible Verse: "The Lord is gracious and compassion-ate, slow to anger and rich in love" (Psalm 145:8).

GOD SHOWS US HOW TO LOVE OTHERS.

Name: _____

FRiENDSHiP FOOD

Preschoolers love to play with their food, so let 'em! Bring out some fruit-flavored cereal rings and some red string licorice, and get ready to make lots of bracelets. (Your child will want to make more than one!) Let your child slip the cereal rings onto pieces of string licorice, just the way he or she would thread beads. For each cereal "bead" that your child adds, have him or her tell a way to show God's love. When your child has finished the bracelet, tie the ends of the licorice together, and let your child decide who will receive the bracelet. (If the strings of licorice are long, your preschooler can make necklaces!) Have your child distribute the bracelets as a way of show-ing God's love to others.

SHiNE YOUR LiGHT

Find a paper cup that's large enough to fit over a flashlight. When it's dark in the evening, let your child shine the flashlight on the ceiling. Talk about how a light in the darkness makes us feel good and safe. Then let your child hide the light by placing the cup over the end of the flashlight. Ask your child what it would be like to live without God's love. Next give your child a ballpoint pen and let him or her poke holes in the cup to let the light spill out. Each time your child pokes a hole, have him or her tell the name of a person who needs to know about God's love. Finally, join with your child in praying for all of the people that were mentioned, and ask God for help in showing his love to others.

Bug Buddies

Today your child learned that fireflies shine as a way of talking to (and finding) other firefly friends. Fireflies can also remind us to shine God's love to everyone around us!

Bug Beats

I Have Decided to Love

(sung to the tune of "I Have Decided")

I have decided to love my friends.
I have decided to love my friends.
I have decided to love my friends.
God tells me to; that's what I'll do.

I have decided to love all others.
I have decided to love all others.
I have decided to love all others.
God tells me to; that's what I'll do.

Copyright © Group Publishing, Inc. www.groupvbs.com